AF231248

The Autism Today Foundation

The Autism Today Foundation works to create a world where autistic individuals are understood, supported, and included. We provide families, caregivers, and communities with clear information, practical tools, and guidance that help improve everyday life for autistic people.

We believe every autistic person has unique strengths and deserves access to opportunities that let them thrive. Through awareness programs, advocacy, and community partnerships, the foundation promotes respect, acceptance, and meaningful participation in schools, workplaces, and society.

Our mission is to support autistic individuals in living full and authentic lives while helping build a future that values neurodiversity.

www.autismtoday.com

Little Rainman Too!

Autism Through the Eyes of My Child

Revised Edition | Neurodiversity Affirming

Foreword by Temple Grandin

ISBN: 978-0-9831308-1-9

Exceptional Resources Publishing

4430, Aaron Place, Boulder Colorado 80303

LITTLE RAINMAN

Autism - through the eyes of a child
by: Karen L. Simmons

When I wrote Little Rainman in the 90s, most books on autism were clinical and focused on challenges. I wanted to share a story from the heart, from the inside out.

People often ask about the title. Back then, the movie Rain Man was a cultural touchstone, and we hoped the name would help the story reach more families who were just beginning to navigate this journey.

Thankfully, times have changed. We now embrace that autism isn't something to be "fixed." It is a beautiful variation of the human experience.

Autistic individuals offer the world unique perspectives, reminding the rest of us of the true meaning of patience, understanding, and love.

Dedication

For Jonathan, who opened my eyes to a different and beautiful way of seeing the world. For every autistic and neurodivergent child, whose voices remind us that diversity is a strength. And for the families, friends, and teachers who choose patience, kindness, and love.

After my near-death experience in 1994, I felt guided to write a book. I first thought it would be about that experience, but no words came. In August 1995, at my first autism conference, everything shifted. As I listened, I felt chills and a strong sense of inspiration. In that moment, I knew this was the story I was meant to tell. The words flowed easily, and I still say the book was written through me, not by me.

When Little Rainman was created in the 1990s, autism was not well understood. Most stories were told by professionals and focused mainly on difficulties. I wanted to offer something different, a view from the heart.

Acknowledgments

To my family, past and present, who gave me strength and encouragement. To my children, each of whom has taught me something special. To Jonathan, for sharing his light and perspective. To my sweet sister, Susan Simmons and my loving late mother, Mitzi Briehn, and the wonderful Robert Woodbury for doing much of the artwork. To my husband Ron, who continues to support me through this journey. To my parents, siblings, and friends who believed in me and this work. A great big thank you also to my wonderful volunteers, Samara Ali, Kasun Priyashantha for providing their participation for editing, graphic design, artwork and thought process that went into this book.

I am thankful to the teachers, therapists, speakers, professionals and community members who supported Jonathan along the way. And I am especially grateful to autistic self-advocates, whose courage and honesty have changed how the world sees autism.

I am thankful to the teachers, therapists, speakers, professionals and community members who supported Jonathan along the way. And I am especially grateful to autistic self-advocates, whose courage and honesty have changed how the world sees autism. Finally, to all autistic children and adults: this book is for you. The world is brighter because you are in it.

Foreword
by
Temple Grandin

I have always really liked the original "Little Rainman" book. It does an excellent job of showing how one type of autistic mind, the visual thinker, works. I also really liked how the illustrations were redone; they looked really super nice, and they were beautiful.

I have even used some of the images from this book in my own presentations and slides over the years. I especially like the pictures of the movie projector inside the head because it shows how some of us think in full, detailed pictures in our minds. The other illustration I've used is the one showing the boxes inside the head, sorting things into different categories. Categories are exactly how I think.

This book really illustrates thinking in pictures and how categories are made, which is key for visual thinkers like me. However, it is important to remember that autism is very diverse. There are other types of thinkers out there, like the mathematical or pattern thinkers, and the word-fact thinkers who memorize everything about a favorite topic, like a sports team or every part number in an auto parts store.

For the visual thinker, "Little Rainman Too" really hits the mark. It provides a simple, direct way to explain how this kind of mind operates. That's why I recommend it.

Why I Asked Temple Grandin to Write the Foreword

Before Little Rainman was published, I attended my first autism conference in Toronto. I was nervous and unsure of what to expect. In the elevator, I unexpectedly found myself standing beside Temple Grandin, who was presenting there along with Dr. Ivar Lovaas.

I was holding a simple manila folder with the unbound manuscript of Little Rainman, filled with hope and the dream of helping others understand autism from a child's point of view. Gathering my courage, I asked Temple if she would look at it.

I did not hear back, so I sent the manuscript to Future Horizons, hoping but not expecting much. Six months later, Wayne Gilpin, the President, contacted me with the news that they wanted to publish it. At the time, they had only thirty-four autism titles, and suddenly Little Rainman became one of them.

Months later, I met Temple again at another conference. When I asked if she had ever read my manuscript, she laughed and said, "You are the one who forgot to put your name on your material. Never forget your contact information. I wanted to ask if I could use your pictures in my presentations."

That moment stayed with me. What began as a nervous elevator encounter became a friendship and a valued professional connection. Today, Temple and I still share a commitment to helping others understand autism, and I am humbled that she continues to use some of the illustrations from Little Rainman in her talks.

If you are reading this book, you may want to learn more about autism. The definitions below reflect our understanding at the time of writing, but autism is always evolving. For updated information, you are invited to visit autismtoday.com and autismtoday.org.

What is Autism

Autism, or Autism Spectrum Disorder, is a developmental difference that shapes how people communicate and experience the world. Some autistic individuals use spoken language, while others communicate through gestures, writing, or technology. All communication is valid.

Many autistic people have heightened sensitivity to sound, light, texture, or movement. Others show strong memory, creativity, or deep focus on specific interests.

Autism is a spectrum because it includes many different ways of thinking and interacting. No two autistic people are alike. Each person has their own strengths and challenges.

What Causes Autism

Older beliefs wrongly blamed parents or family dynamics. Today we know autism has biological and genetic foundations. It is nobody's fault. It is a lifelong neurodevelopmental difference and a natural part of human diversity.

Autistic people deserve acceptance, respect, and the chance to thrive. This updated edition keeps Jonathan's voice while using more affirming language, reflecting what autistic self-advocates continue to teach us.

For more information and updates, visit ***autismtoday.com***

LiTTLE RAINMAN
autism today
Autism - through the eyes of a child
by Karen L. Simmons

x

If you are a parent or professional in the autism world, this book is for you. My commitment to helping others understand autism began decades ago, when a doctor told me, "Your son has autism; he may end up in an institution. Bring him back in a year." That moment of despair became my inspiration to find and share resources, ensuring I didn't miss his most critical years for intervention. Thirty years later, that inspiration drives me still.

Little Rainman Too is my 15th book, and I've spoken at over 75 conferences worldwide. Recognizing that autism knows no boundaries, I founded Autism Today Foundation and Autism Today Foundation Canada to support parents and professionals everywhere. Whether in North America, Africa, or India, the challenges are the same, and autism is a lifelong condition.

My goal is to emphasize that early intervention is key to helping children reach their full potential.

Much love to the autism community

Karen Simmons
Mom of 7,
Founder, Autism Today

Contents

XIV

Who Am I?

My name is Jonathan. I'm autistic (aw-tis-tik). My nose looks the same as other people's and my ears and eyes do too. Except that I can see and hear a lot better than most people.

My brain works its own way. Some things I do better, like reading and copying; other things I find it harder, like making friends. I need help with learning to do some things.

There aren't many people like me, maybe more than most people realize, so I am very unique. I will always need to learn how to navigate a world not always built for me, which comes naturally to most other people.

2

Sensory Issue (s)

When I was a baby I did not like to be touched or held, even by my parents. I would cry when I was picked up. My grandparents thought this was a bit odd, but everyone else didn't think much of it.

Back then, when I was between around three years old, I was fascinated with circles, and spinning my body around. I liked to spin things around and around, really fast.

My parents had to re-connect the chandelier three times because I literally spinned it out of the ceiling. Also I would climb into the dishwasher and spin the bottom of it.

Repetition

Mom and I would play an exercise game. She would extend one leg in the air and say "Circles in the air, circles in the air, switch" over and over again.

I loved this game and would laugh very loud. I would always put the same leg in the air, though, not switching to the other.

 We don't play this any more cause Mom says I get too attached to the game.

Stimming

I like to spin around in circles. Mom says a lot of people with autism (like me) like to spin. We like wheels on cars, walking in circles, flapping our hands in the air, or even rocking back and forth.

I also like to sing loud saying wee-wee-wee. It just makes me feel good to do this. Grown up people have a name for this. They call it "stimming". All I know is that it makes me feel good even though mom says most people think it is silly.

Touch

When I was younger, I didn't like to be touched because my skin was so sensitive. It would almost hurt to be touched, especially when I wasn't initiating the touching. People thought I wanted my own space.

I couldn't stand crowds and didn't like to be with people. Of course I like people, it's just that I don't show it the same way most people do. I like to stay with people a lot more nowadays.

Physical Space

I can stay in a room full of people for up to fifteen minutes! When I stay around people I sometimes stay safe inside my own head. It's like I have my safe space just for me.

 Most people have a two foot space around themselves when they don't want people to be too close to them; well, my space is about ten feet minimum! Being in crowds is still my least favorite thing to do.

Vision

I have a hard time thinking about more than one thing at a time. That's probably why I don't like to look into peoples' eyes when they are speaking to me. I just don't see any reason to look at them when they are talking.

It seems uncomfortable for me to do this. This continues into my older years, even to this day. I'm almost five years old now. It's like I would rather hear what their eyes are telling me. I sort of look at them out of the corner of my eyes and they think it's creepy.

Even though my vision is 20/20 I think something might be wrong with my eyes because I have a hard time catching a ball, and I accidentally bump into people lots of times. They get upset with me and sometimes cry. All I can say is "sorry". Mom is going to have my eyes checked out by a special eye doctor.

Facial Expression(s)

I sometimes don't understand what people mean by the expression on their faces because I don't know what it means. Maybe someone is angry with me or dont want to play with me but I can't tell.

Older people seem to think I should automatically know if someone doesn't want to play with me. I don't get it until it is too late.

There is a girl in my class who is always smiling and acts like the other kids, at least I think she does. She's always by herself and kids pick on her, like they do with me too!

I think they are mean to her but I don't know why.

Sound(s)

Sounds are another thing. I can hear helicopters in the air before my brothers and sisters do. I say, "What's that noise?" When there are a lot of people in a room making a lot of racket, I sometimes have to leave the room.

Also, I can't stand it when the blender is on.

I say, there is too much noise. Mom told me that sounds from bright light bulbs really bother some autistic people. The humming drives them crazy.

They just can't stand staying and listening to that loud buzzing sound. At night, the air conditioner vent in my room keeps me awake until very late. It bugs me a a lot so I know how they feel.

Whirr
Humm
can't touch this!
15

Coordination

Most recently, my mom had to take me out of tap dancing class. I kept mixing my feet up. When the class used their left foot to do their shuffle step, I used my right foot.

It was so confusing, and the music and tapping was way too loud! I had to cover my ears with my hands to stand it. When we were marching, I slipped on my taps and fell.

That's when I started crying from the inside of my heart.

I was embarrassed and didn't want my tears to show so I kept them inside of me. Mom took me out and we didn't go back inside. She took me out for good!

Atypical Boundaries

Right afterwards, outside of the classroom, I saw a little girl. I wanted to see if anything was written on the back of her shirt like my shirt was. She wouldn't let me take off her sweater.

Mom told me not to take someone else's clothes off that I don't even know. I still don't understand. I was trying to get to know her and to see her back.

I also like to kiss people that I like. They will back away from me like I am sick or something. I guess I shouldn't do that.

Irritability

Mom also signed me up for Tae Kwon Do. I loved it so much but Ma'am and Sir (the teachers) got upset with me. I couldn't hold still and kept spinning around in circles and humming.

The other kids kept staring at me. I just had a stomach ache and had to go pee. I was upset with Ma'am too cause she didn't understand me. Anyway, I kept kicking everybody for fun, even my brothers and sisters. So, they told my mom to take me out and maybe I could try again next year when I am six. I'm sure sad about it.

Color(s)

My favorite color used to be orange. Now it is blue. I really don't like red or yellow or black. Mostly I like light blue and dark blue and green.

NAIL POLISH REMOVER
DIAPER PAIL
PAINT
BLEACH
SIN
LOVE
Ecstacy
Mitzi Briehn

I have a new friend now named Cody. He is autistic too. We really liked each other a lot. It was like we were on the same wavelength.

He thought a lot like me and it was hard for him to leave my house. I keep thinking of that guy. His mom says that he doesn't like bright colors at all. But he does like blue, gray and darker colors just like me.

Scent(s)

Some smells really bug me, like a stinky bathroom or something. Of course that bugs mostly everybody but I really can't stand it.

Perfume, gasoline and even some people stink so much I used to not be able to stay in the same room with them. Now that I am used to more smells, it is easier to be around it.

Cody, my new friend, can't stand the smell of tomato sauce to this day and he is already eleven years old.

He is so funny, he calls his mom Gail instead of mom and so do his brother and sister.

Relationship(s)

Getting to know people is kind of like automatic glass doors. When you run up too fast, they don't open up. I think this is true with kids and grown ups. I have to be very careful not to make people think I am weird.

Fixation(s)

Sometimes the wallpaper on the wall starts to come off. I just can't stand when it is like that, some on and some off. I have to peel it off. I just have to. One piece at a time until it's all gone.

25

I like the way it feels, and it bugs me when it isn't all in place too.

Also, it sounds really neat to rip it off. Dad is having a fit but I think it is cool. I guess he'll just paint the wall or something instead of wallpaper.

Perseveration

I like to say things over and over again, over and over again, over and over again. Then I start to laugh.

If my brother says "What do you think you're doin?" Then I will say "What do you think you're doin" right back to him. Mom told me this is called (Per-sev-ur-a-shun) because it sounds the same.

Because I am autistic, I like to copy people this way. I also watch the same movies over and over too.

Q

Sensory

Another thing that bugs me are my clothes. If they are scratchy or uncomfortable, then all that I can think of is getting those clothes off! I would rather wear no clothes at all if it's not too cold out.

Clothes can wreck my day at school if they are wrong. I feel all tied up in knots if I have the wrong clothes on or those inside tags on my neck.

I have my favorite outfit to wear. I wear it in the daytime and to sleep in. It feels so soft and it doesn't have any hard things in it. I would wear it every day if it didn't need washing.

When I first learned to walk, my steps were out of balance.

I also went down stairs one step at a time. I did this by putting my left foot on the step below me and bringing my right foot down beside my left foot on the same step.

I still do this. I feel like I might lose my balance going down the stairs, so I'd rather slide down the banister.

One time when I was just three I decided to go for a walk down the street. I had my diapers on and nothing else.

There was snow on the ground and it felt good so I kept going, all the way to the big road.

Some lady picked me up in her car and drove me around the neighborhood. The car stopped near my house and mom came running to see if it was me in the car.

The lady seemed very mad at mom and mom was very mad at me. I guess I should have told her I was going.

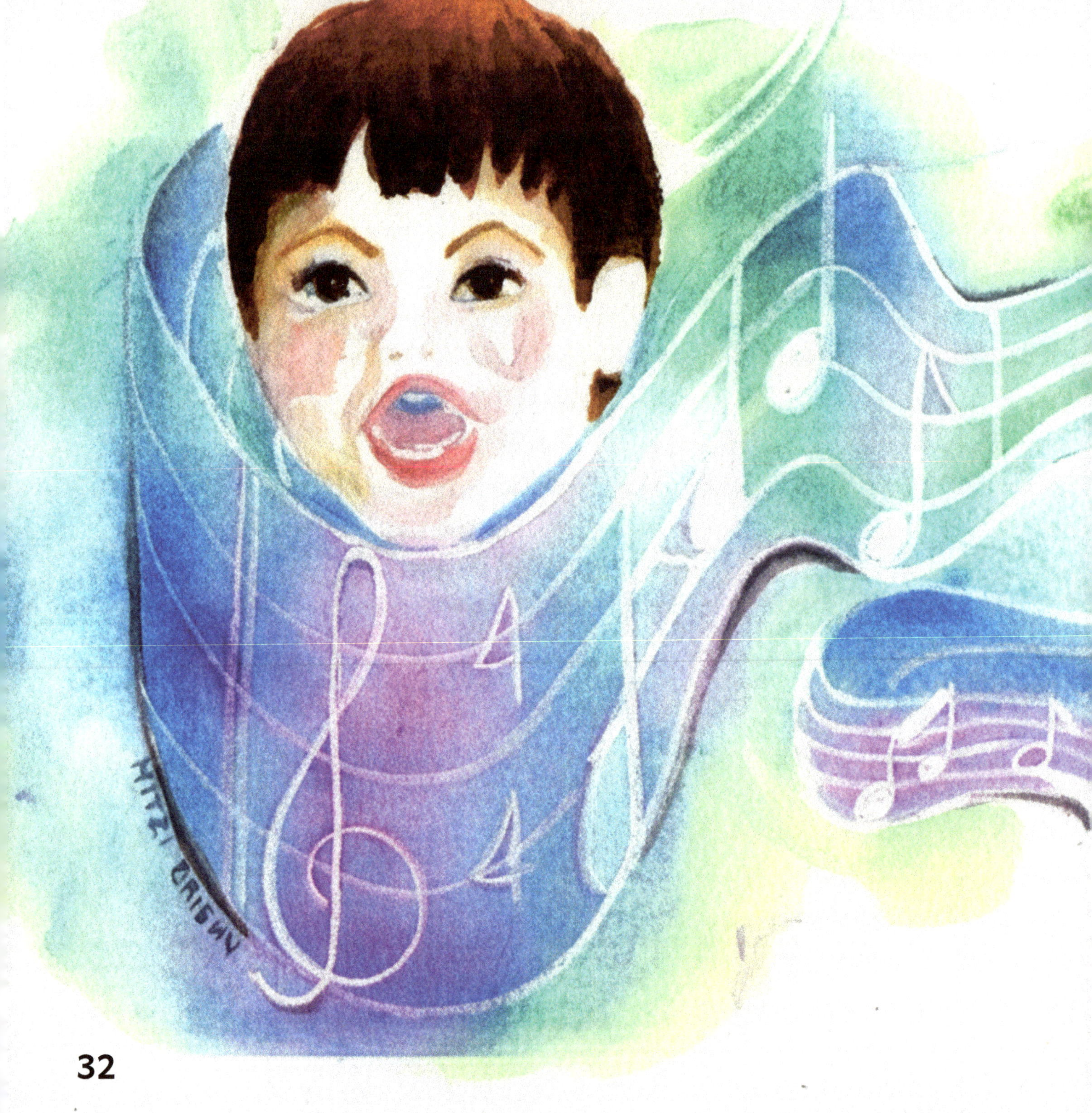

Music

I love music and can remember a song backwards and forwards. An example: "I think you're A one grade a, beloved and beautiful, capable, caring, delightful dependable, etc. but then I got sick of it and said no, no, no, no, stop stop stop…"

The tune goes around in my head for hours. My music teacher tells my mom I can hit perfect notes and have great rhythm.

Sometimes I forget where I am and continue to hum a tune even when a lot of people are around. People think this is a bit silly. I think it's okay though.

RECYCLE
RECYCLE NOW

I began reading (out loud) when I was two and a half. Mom thinks I actually was reading sooner. My first word was recycle. My parents and I were at the park when we walked by this truck that said recycle. I said ru-si-kul. They looked at each other in disbelief!

In time more words kept coming. I read everywhere I go, even the writing on bathroom walls. I went to a party and all I could say were the letters E - X - I - T out the door over and over and continued to go out the door around the side and back into the room.

It was the only way I could stand being around all those people. I did this all night at that party. My parents didn't know what to do with me.

EXIT
EXIT

Reading And Talking

Every night I read myself to sleep with books that my ten-year-old sister lets me keep. Mom says that some kids with autism don't read and some don't talk. Mom thinks they must understand anyway, they just think different than most other people. So do I!

I like to read books about the body to help me go to sleep.

One day my older brother Matt was complaining about having a stomach ache. He said he didn't know why he had it. I said "I get it, the food gets carried to other parts of your body and that gives you a stomach ache." I think he knows now.

I get very upset with people when they don't understand me. I say "You're not listening" or "You got it all wrong, that's the wrong answer". Mom can tell in my voice if I'm upset.

At least I can tell someone what is bothering me. I might get mad and push someone away or not talk to them, or cry. That doesn't mean I don't like them though.

Mom says that some autistic people don't talk or read and the only way they talk to others is by pointing to pictures. I am sure glad I can talk. If I didn't maybe I might get too upset and frustrated. I already get frustrated and kick sometimes if I couldn't talk or read, it would be harder.

I like to know what is going to happen ahead of time or I get upset. That's one reason I like to watch movies over and over again. If I know what is going to happen, I'm happy,

But if I am not sure what to expect then somebody, like my grown up helper tells me I do some bizarre things, like throwing tantrums and dropping on the ground.

She tells me not to do that anymore.

I also may make noises or say something I heard in a movie once.

Baby Shark and Paw Patrol used to be my two favorite shows. I would stay glued to them for the entire show and want to watch it again and again.

Now that I'm almost five, I like cartoons and other kid movies. I like to watch them over and over again, maybe fifty times. This way, I can memorize all the words and music.

It makes me feel good to know the beginning and the end of each tape and also to know what comes next. Movies I can predict; people, I cannot.

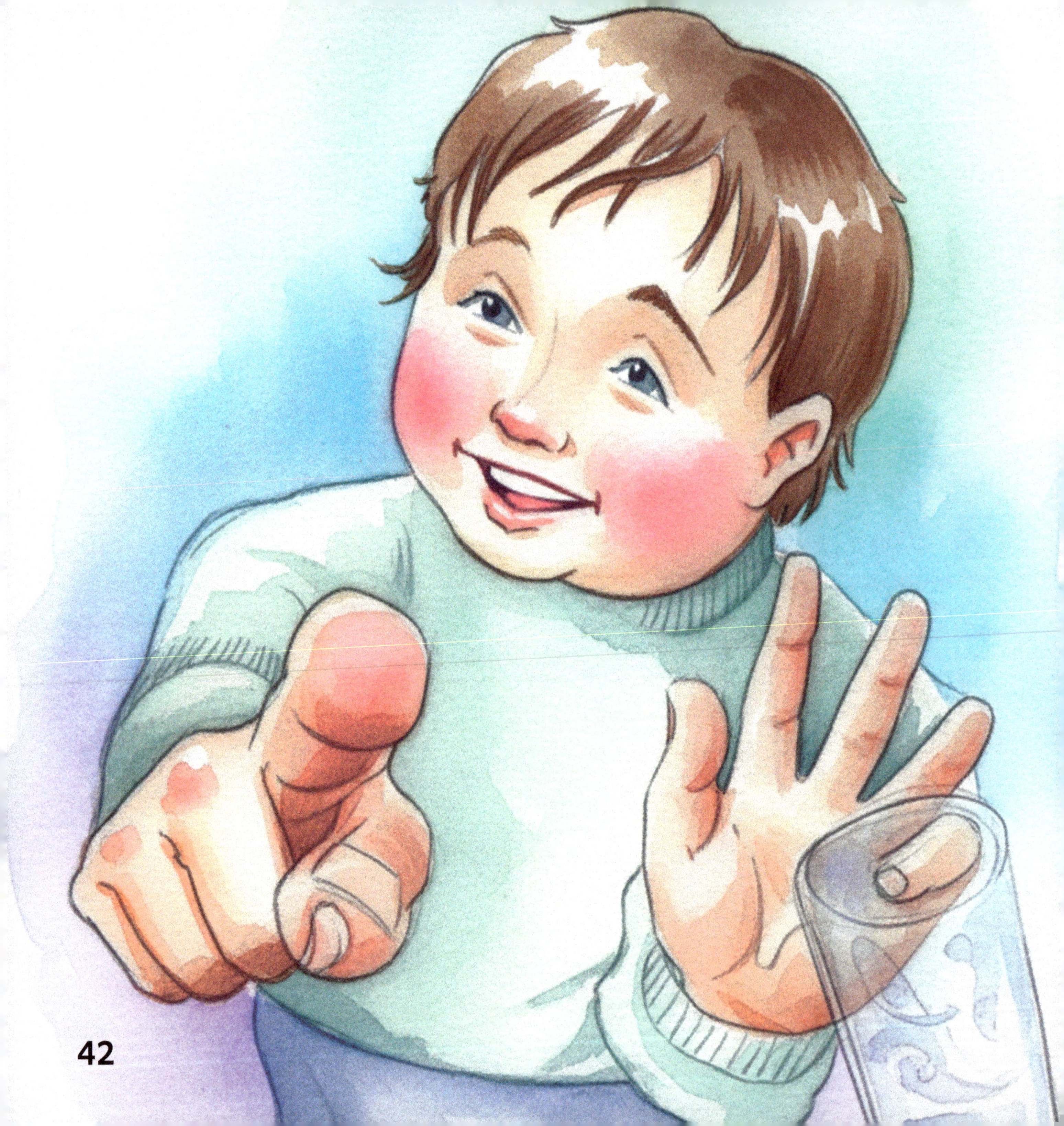

Foods

I like food but some foods I wouldn't even like to touch. Especially if it's all mixed together. I don't know what is in that stuff. It just looks too mixed up for me.

Foods that I can pick up are usually good because they don't have sauce. Mushy foods, like bananas, are yuk.

My big sister doesn't like her foods to touch. She won't eat it if her peas touch her corn. I think she's a bit picky.

Some drinks I don't like either. Mom says that a lot of autistic people are a picky eaters. Of course, other people can be too!

Computers

My computer is my favorite thing to play with. I think like it does and it thinks like I do. It makes me happy to be playing it, all the time if I could. We both think the same, exactly to the point.

The computer's and my brain picks out just one piece of information at a time to focus on, not more. That's why the computer and I are so much alike. I can play on for hours. In fact, I feel like I need to play on it sometimes just to calm down.

I play Minecraft and other cool games that everyone else likes. I can also get hung up on just entering and exiting the computer. This happened a lot when I first got interested in computers at the age of two.

46

In one computer game we flush things through the toilet to a guy named Hoagy. He is the fat guy in the program. Even when I wasn't playing with the computer, I used to say "I'm Hoagy, the fat guy!"

Mom says I get things that are not real mixed up with real things. I love to flush "things" to Hoagy. Mom has had to call the plumber many times.

One time I really scared my mom when I was Sonic the Hedgehog. I stood on her balcony and said "Sonic wants to fly!" She thought I was going to jump.

Mitzi Briehn

At the time I thought it would be fun cause I saw it on TV. After, mom told me I could get killed if I jumped. I understand now. Instead I like to try and go down the laundry chute.

Mom doesn't let me do that either though. She says I would get stuck and then she would have to call 911. I try when she is not around.

Once I got stuck in a big plant pot. My sister poured vaseline on the edges till I finally slipped out. After I stopped crying she said 'it was like the pot was giving birth". I don't know what that means.

I enjoy doing the things that I like to do, like reading and computing. Some things are easy for me to do like counting up to 200, playing computers, video games, reading and music.

I also want to be liked and have friends. Friendships are hard for me. Just getting along with kids is very difficult.

Playing

When I play with someone, I can't talk with the kid and play at the same time. I like to do one or the other. Sometimes they just go away.

Sometimes people look at me silly when I say "Hi, I'm Richie Rich, the richest kid in the world." It is fun for me to pretend in this way. I like to be "Richie" until I find another character in a movie or in a computer game that I can become.

Just like the other night when we went to see Murmel Murmel, Mortimer Munch. Then I was Mortimer and Mom was Mortimer's Mom. Lately I haven't wanted to be anyone at all except me. For Halloween I am going to be a plain boy!

My feelings get hurt very easy and sometimes I cry and tell someone that I am very sad. Sometimes I believe people too much. They tell me something I believe and they trick me.

I like kids to like me and I like some kids too, but some are very mean. I know I'm different and I just want to know how and fit in.

Community

I might do a lot to get someone to like me. Sometimes to the point of being stupid. Mom told me about a boy that was sixteen years old. He was autistic.

Another guy told this boy to get on the floor and bark like a dog. The boy did because he thought he would be his friend then. A bunch of guys just laughed at him and hurt his feelings.

His teacher told him to tell those boys to leave him alone. He didn't do anything silly like that again. Real friends wouldn't ask him to make a fool of himself. I hope I don't fall for something like that when I get older.

WOOF!

I got kicked off the bus because I cut the bus seat. I wasn't good at talking those days but excellent at typing so the principal made me write an apology letter to the driver because I damaged her stuff.

I told her a kid was throwing jello pudding (with the lids off) at me and would jump from seat to seat to get at me. The reason I cut her seats was because I was frustrated and had to do something. I said "sorry for cutting her seats".

My grown up helper got hurt by an autistic teenager who hit her. He broke her hand. He was mad because he was hungry and he wanted food right then.

I also like to do what I want to do when I want to do it. I feel this way but I'm learning to accept "no" for an answer sometimes. Grown-ups need to have a lot of patience with me. I can get lost without rigid rules.

Timing

When I was younger, dinner had to be on the table exactly at 5:00 PM or my parents couldn't get me to the table without a fight. They watched the clock so when the time was at 5:00 on the dot, we all would sit down together.

I talk differently than other people. My mom tries to correct me when I say I don't want "no" mayonnaise, but I know differently. (at least my way seems right). She will repeat it her way until I finally memorize her way but I still don't understand what makes her way right.

When I go try to sleep at night the helper asked me why I couldn't sleep. I said 'well, when the bed squeaks that means the springs need to be oiled."

They got a new mattress that didn't make those noises so I could sleep.

Also, some kid call me stupid and weird and other names because I talk slower than they do. I think it just takes me longer to think of an answer than other people. It is because I wasn't already thinking about it. I was probably thinking about something else.

My brother must think my brain has a lot of compartments like boxes in it. It's because I have to focus really hard on one thing at a time, since so many other things are happening at the same time.

My thoughts have to jump from box to box. He thinks I can't hear him when I really can. It's just that I am too working on what I want to do something else.

I try to picture exactly what people are saying. When someone says "it's raining cats and dogs", I look up to the sky to see if any animals are coming down.

Sometimes I get upset from all the stuff going on. Everything is coming at me from all directions, and I feel like running away. Sometimes I do and I forget to tell anyone.

One time I decided to bring my little brother, Stephen, to climb a chimney at someone else's house. Mom caught us and got really mad at me.

Another time Mom was driving five of us kids back from computer class. I thought Tetrus was a really cool computer game.

My brother, Matt started to scream when I decided to play and hit him on his head with a book. Mom said it seemed like a harmless game until that happened.

A few months ago, we were playing a video game called "Lost Vikings". They played with knives inside

MITZI BRIEHN

the game so I wanted to do that also when I got home. I went upstairs to get the biggest one I could find, so I could kill the enemy. After all, Isn't that what we're supposed to do, get rid of the bad guys?

When I was older,Dad took us to the ranch. He was letting us practice with real swords and I accidentally cut my little brother's finger. He had to go to the hospital to stitch his finger back.

Mom was so mad at dad when she heard about it.

If I don't want to go someplace, like school, I say "School is closed, I think it is all locked up". My way of saying this is different than my brother's. He would say "I don't want to go to school!"

I'm glad I have my sisters and brothers. It forces me to get along with kids even when I don't want to.

SCHOOL
CLOSED

They teach me a lot and we love each other. They tell their friends how I am different and unique.

I even went to my brothers grade three class and read a book in front of the class. Matt, Kim and Christina were so proud of me. Some kids understand about me and some don't. I like to fit in and play but some kids are nice to me and others aren't.

Truth is, I'm just like everybody. I want friends and want to be liked too even though it may seem like I don't care.

I want to be loved and accepted for who I am and never be made fun of. I like to fit in. Mom tells me I am different and special. She also says I am very smart. I get the feeling that I truly am because of how I get treated by some people.

What I really want in life is to be happy, have lots of fun and for people to like me.

Jonathan S.

64

Mitzi Brehn